It began on a dating site. Well,
what story doesn't n~~~~~
was looking throu
reviewing pictures
thoroughly throug
matches in the ab
and I paused over a photo of a trip
to the zoo with this one woman and
what I figured was her boyfriend.
Some of her contacts had left
appreciative messages, that I
supposed she also attached to her
pictures to get more attention, and
it was one of those that caught my
eye. Not the message, which just
said "Gorgeous!" (which indeed the
photo was): the name. Imma
Stokes. I knew it was her, even
without the little avatar photo of
her, which proved it beyond doubt.
It was her all right. Imma. I felt a
tingling going through my whole
body. Suddenly I was back there,
back at the time we got along,

loved each other in those mad last weeks of the summer. The time I had tried so hard to shut out of my mind but had never quite managed to. The time I always went back to in my daydreams and my fantasies. Imma.

I was working in my design studio when my phone buzzed. Glancing at the screen, I saw the single letter 'M.' Mistress! I didn't let it ring a second time. From the other end, I heard the smoky, sensual voice say "Come," and I nearly did right there. She hung up, not needing to say anything more. I knew where to go. I left my studio early, got in my car and drove. It had been nearly three weeks since I last heard from her and I ached to see her again.

Some may think it strange to be so obsessed with this woman who I knew nearly nothing about. I do know that she's not a made up dominant. And I mean super dominant. She doesn't bother with being fake, didn't have to. self-confident, higher poise, prefers to be treated like a "person" and not like a "woman", prefers independence and "standing on her own feet", lack feelings of inferiority, and generally she doesn't care for concessions that imply she is inferior, weak or that she needs. Imma had it all!!

Lainey threw her head back as jolts of pleasure and pain burst through her body. Repeatedly, Imma's hand landed on Lainey's bare ass, and she felt the stinging sensation melt into a familiar burn. Her stress faded with each blow.

She had followed her dominant lovers instructions, removing her panties in the taxi on the way back from the airport. Moments after arriving, she found herself over Imma's lap. Lainey still wore her business suit, her skirt pulled up to expose her round ass. Part of her felt this was wrong. It's not appropriate for a respected business woman to willingly take a spanking over her lovers knee. But that just made it so much more desirable. To say Lainey wanted her strict hand would be an under-statement. With every fiber of her being, she needed this release. The weight of her day melted away as her ass moved with each slap.

Sensing she'd had enough, Imma helped Lainey to her seat. With Lainey's skirt still hiked up around her hips, Imma rubbed Lainey's ass and felt its radiant heat. Imma smiled confidently at Lainey as she took in the sight. Lainey still had her hair up in a neat creation, but a few deep brown tufts had escaped during the spanking. Expecting to end up exposed before Imma, Lainey had neatly trimmed her pubic hair, leaving only a narrow strand. Imma seemed to like it that way.

"Now, take off your clothes," Imma said, her voice demanding.

Lainey unbuttoned her jacket with unsteady fingers. How could she still feel so vulnerable around Imma after all these years? It was a sensual wonder. After dropping the jacket on the floor, her blouse followed, leaving her with just her skirt around her hips and a black lace bra, which held up her straining breasts. High heels emphasized her toned legs. Imma nodded towards her bra, and Lainey reached behind to unclasp it. Her tits fell free, swaying heavily before her dominant lover. Imma looked pleased as she studied them, and Lainey invitingly pushed her chest out for Imma's benefit.

Lainey lowered her gaze as Imma stood. Imma began circling, and moving her strong hands over Lainey's delicate skin. Lainey flinched as Imma suddenly slapped her tender cheeks. Standing behind her, one hand traveled up her body. A soft moan escaped her mouth as Imma reached Lainey's breast. Imma felt its weight in her hand before softly pinching her pink nipple. Lainey savored the familiar smell of Imma's erotic perfume as Imma traveled Lainey's body with her hands.

When Imma turned Lainey's body, she marveled at the weakness in her legs as their eyes met. Imma's gaze was demanding, but warmth shined through. Lainey knew what was expected, and sank to the floor. Unzipping Imma's pants with her teeth, keeping eye contact with Imma at all times to be sure her dominant was pleased Lainey pulled out Imma's firm double sided delight cock. Lainey looked up at Imma with pleading eyes, and

Imma nodded. Leaning in, Lainey took it between her lips. It grew even harder inside her mouth, and the sloppy sounds of her worship filled the room. The skirt around her hips and high heels were a reminder of the stature of the woman who now submissively knelt on the floor, her ass reddened from the spanking.

Imma pulled away before Lainey brought forth her climax. Sometimes, Imma would finish in Lainey's mouth or on her face with vanilla yogurt that she inserted in the chamber and released when she felt pleased with a remote that came with the rock hard rocket. Then Imma enjoyed sitting back and watching as Lainey pleasured her own body. Lainey loved touching herself for Imma . It left her feeling like a submissive slut.

But, having been apart for nearly two weeks, they both craved the entrance of Imma's powerful cock into Lainey's needy core.

"Get on the couch," Imma commanded.

Lainey obeyed. Positioned face down against the cushion, her ass became the highest point of reference. She reached between her legs and felt the wetness as she invitingly parted her lips for Imma . Silently, Lainey remained in that position as Imma slowly undressed.

The couch moved as Imma knelt behind Lainey. Imma placed the tip of her cock at Lainey's entrance, and with one steady motion, pushed deep inside her. Lainey wailed in gratification. With a mounting force, Imma moved in and out of Lainey's trembling frame. Soon, Imma's hips slammed domineeringly against Lainey's tender ass. Lainey's moans escalated in tempo and volume, as Imma began slapping her cheeks. Ecstasy overtook Lainey and she quaked as the orgasm took her body. Her dominant lover continued to spank her as she screamed through her climax. Imma moaned from her double sided delight as she pressed herself against Lainey and released a seemingly endless flow inside her contracting enfold.

Imma collapsed on top of Lainey, softly kissing her neck and face. Their bliss transcended words. Imma's hands tenderly caressed Lainey's spent body. Eventually, Lainey left and cleaned up. Her ass was still glowing upon her return, with several imprints from Imma's hand visible.

Everything was overwhelming. Every part of Imma's body was aware of Lainey's, of how Imma could manipulate Lainey to do whatever she wished. Even with this power over Lainey, there was nothing but consideration for what Imma wanted, each and everything that Imma had talked to Lainey about was encompassed in this encounter. The teasing, the blindfold, the structure of it all. Right down to the placing of Lainey in whatever position that Imma wished. Lainey didn't want to have to think about anything but Imma's commands or the sensations Imma caused, letting everything else melt into nothingness.

After three weeks of talking, emailing and instant messaging, Imma and I were finally going to meet -- in real time, in real life. I was excited and a little nervous, but most of all I was afraid it was going to be like all my other online dating site matches -- disappointing. How is it possible a woman can look and sound so good online yet be the total opposite in person? I sat through more than a few dinners wondering what the hell I was doing there and trying to figure out how I could end the night early without seeming rude. The only bad thing about 'making it an early night' was I would have to deal with that awkward goodbye moment sooner. That moment where you have to explain that you would like to see her again, but as friends...that you really liked her and enjoyed the evening, but just didn't feel the spark.

But with Imma I was hoping it would be different. I was banking on my multiple experiences of bad dates to help me do a better job of screening before we actually met. We had spoken on the phone so I already knew I liked her voice. It was direct and convincing and I liked the way she would pause before she would share something personal about herself. It was as if she was considering how vulnerable she wanted to be with a woman she had never met. Some women would bare their souls in the first 10 minutes. By the end of the first conversation I knew about every bad relationship they ever had, their fucked-up childhoods and their hopes for the future, which by that point I knew would not include me. But Imma would only give me little bits and pieces at a time. It wasn't that she was being secretive or shut down, but careful. She knew that once the words were out she couldn't take them back. She was smart, too. We could talk about anything, and did. You could tell she read a lot, her opinions were well-thought out. She was articulate and knowledgeable. She could look at any issue from a lot of different angles and would challenge me, something most people never did. I liked that about her.

Obsession

I felt the sexual heat run through my body and settle in my pussy. How could I feel so aroused, just from a series of glances?

Imma and I had found a restaurant close to the newly renovated convention centre. It had looked a little upmarket for us but the table d'hôte menu had been surprisingly within our budget. And in that early afternoon time zone between the end of business lunch and the start of happy hour, it was relatively empty.

The morning workshop had gone on for far too long and the only relief from the droning speaker had been when Imma had started her sexual games. I'm sure a couple of delegates nearby had noticed when she slipped her hand under the hem of my skirt but that sort of thing only encouraged her more.

We'd been an item for a couple of years now, ever since we'd met. One thing had led to another. We'd gone with another group to a pub afterwards and as people had drifted away, Imma had told me she loved brunettes and invited me back to her small bedsit for 'coffee'.

I'd been with other women before, of course, but until I'd felt her fingers and mouth ravaging me, I'd been content to drift between lovers of either gender. She'd devoured me completely and since that night I'd been completely devoted to her.

I'd long ago discovered that the idea of sex in public, with a real danger of being seen, was quite a turn on for her. She was incorrigible in that mood and the long white tablecloth had allowed her to continue her games in the restaurant without being noticed by the few other diners.

Or had we?

It was the woman I could see over Imma's right shoulder who had tuned into our action. I was sure she had. I'd felt her looking at me... probing, searching. She was much older than either of us, in her mid forties, perhaps? A few strands of her dark hair sexily fell across her face and her dress was displaying almost as much of her long toned legs as it was her impressive cleavage.

But it was her eyes that had got to me more than anything. They smoldered.

There wasn't the slightest doubt in my mind that she knew what we were doing. Each time Imma became more adventurous under the table, the woman would smile at me while she flicked a hand through her hair, or ran her tongue across her full lips, or crossed and then uncrossed those long legs, or ran the tip of her finger across her fabulous cleavage...

God, she was a sexy bitch.

I found that I was becoming more turned on by her attention than I actually was by Imma's hand. More accurately, the way those deep eyes smoldered at me made me fantasize that it was her hand under the table, not my girlfriend's.

What the fuck was wrong with me?

I eventually excused myself and headed for the restrooms. A quick freshen up would help me ease the sexual tension I was feeling and then Imma and I would be heading back to register for tomorrow's conference. I'd never been unfaithful in my life, nor did I intend ever to break that resolution, yet by flirting so openly with our eyes, I almost felt that I'd been cheating on my girlfriend. Escaping from that piercing gaze would allow me to calm me down.

The exposed brick walls of the restaurant seemed to be closing in as I headed towards the restrooms, making me realize just how much I had drank while we'd enjoyed our meal. Imma was good with alcohol. I'd never been that way.

Alone in the bathroom, I hurried over to the sink and placed my palms face down on the cool counter. My heart was palpitating. I stared at myself in the mirror, seeing the need in my eyes staring back. As soon as we'd registered I'd take Imma back to the hotel and let her have her wicked way with me. She'd like that.

God, so would I...

My mind began to drift. Whereas Imma was blonde, my first experience of girl-girl sex had been with a brunette, just like the woman in the restaurant. She'd been a similar age, too. Sandra had been a professor at my University and had a reputation for taking a fancy to some of her students. I'd been an innocent in those days of course and had been putty in her hands.

The very first time she'd taken me back to her quarter's at the University, she'd done things to me I'd only seen in porn films. Then she'd introduced me to her strappy. I'd always been curious about what it would be like to be fucked like that by another woman. I bit my lip as the recollection began to overwhelm me. I could almost feel her large strappy thrusting inside me...

The thought of the woman in the restaurant doing the same to me loomed large in my mind. God, sometimes these sexual fantasies just appeared in my mind from nowhere. Sandra been so sweet and so gentle but the woman I'd just been flirting with wouldn't be either. The look in her eyes told me that.

Why the fuck did that thought turn me on so much?

My body trembled. Was I cumming? Without even touching myself? Impossible.

I was dabbing water on my face, starting to pull myself together, when she entered the restrooms. I saw her in the mirror as I glanced up and I felt a shudder of arousal run through my body. I hadn't expected this...

She stood with her back to the door, arms folded across her breasts, just staring at me. Then she spoke.

"I love the pose. Is that for me?"

I realized that I was still half bent forward. That was the position I'd automatically adopt when Sandra entered the room, naked except for her long strappy. A bead of sweat broke out on my forehead and I stood up and turned towards her. Those eyes were burning into me again.

Neither of us spoke for a moment. My hands rested on the counter behind me, holding me up. I felt weak at the knees.

She sauntered across the room, stopping just short of me. She had one meticulously plucked brow raised, the corners of her full lips turned up in amusement, and those dark eyes were sending a message that was impossible to ignore.

"You were waiting for me?"

I shook my head. I needed to get out of there as quickly as I could.

"Of course not."

She raised a hand to my face and when I quickly turned my head to the side, her fingertips caressed my cheek.

"Of course you were. We both know that."

I just stared at her, unsure of how to respond.My nipples were already piercing my thin top and if I let go of the countertop I would crumble in a heap.

"I have to get back to my girlfriend."

She nodded, acknowledging and yet dismissing the thought.

"The blonde? She's cute. But not as cute as you. You're both English?"

I pursed my lips and nodded. I couldn't trust myself to speak. There was something about this woman that crawled inside you and made you sweat. I'd never met anyone with such an incredibly powerful sexual presence.

"My my, what a small world...," she purred. "I grew up in Leeds. They were three of the best years of my life. But perhaps it's just as well that I moved here. If you and I lived close together, you'd be hell on my marriage."

I felt the goosebumps break out on my skin.

"I really need to get back," I said, trying to regain my composure.

She smiled at me, as if challenging me to squeeze past her. She was standing close enough for me to smell her perfume and I could feel her hot breath each time she spoke. When I didn't move, she stepped even closer so that our bodies touched and traced her right index fingertip across the boundary of my left jawline.

"You knew I was watching you, didn't you? Did it turn you on? Is that why you came in here? You knew I would follow you, didn't you?"

I almost creamed my panties at the words. Was this really happening?

"I'm with my girlfriend..."

"I know," she breathed against my mouth. "That makes it all the sexier, don't you think?"

Her arm snaked around my neck. She curled her fingers in my hair and then roughly yanked my head back, tilting it to the side. I gasped in shock. Those full lips were only a fraction away and they looked so inviting...

"I SO love the devoted ones," she murmured as she traced the tip of her tongue along the outside of my lips. "You are going to be so much fun to corrupt."

When her lips pressed against mine, I shamefully responded with all the passion that had been building up over lunch. My body shivered as her snaking tongue invaded my mouth. This was wrong, so wrong. I was with Imma. Anyone could walk in here at any moment.

And yet it was so fucking sexy...

I found myself pinned against the sink behind me as we made out like rabid animals. Her lips were somehow both softer and more demanding than anyone I'd ever been with, woman or man. The feeling of her large breasts pushing against mine, her fingers curled in my hair, was almost more than I could take.

Her whisper was thick and husky as she at last pulled her lips away from mine and whispered in my ear.

"I'm going to touch you. And then I'm going to feed you."

Her teeth nipped my earlobe as her free hand effortlessly eased the hem of my skirt up above the tops of my stockings. I gasped out loud, and she smiled. In an instant her hand was sliding inside my thong. She knew exactly what she was doing and I was completely lost to the red haze engulfing me. Fuck, I was so wet! Her incredible touch skimmed along the ridge of my labia. She teased my clit without touching it, circling the swollen bud.

"Yes?" she whispered, with the slightest tinge of held-back violence.

I panted. This was all of my lewdest fantasies rolled into one.

"Yes..."

"Yes what...?"

"Yes, please..."

She held my head with her left hand tangled in my hair, holding me motionless as she looked in my eyes and smiled at me. When she stiffened two fingers and pushed them into my throbbing pussy, I couldn't contain the scream.

"Godddddddddddd..."

The word came out like a series of reverberations bouncing from the back of my throat. My senses went into overload. When she lightly thumbed my clit she may as well have flipped a detonator. I was cumming and I was cumming hard.

Despite the location, I screamed out again as the most violent of orgasms consumed my body. Erika covered the sound by kissing me again, her lips wet and soft. And then I felt her fingers against my mouth... feeding me my own juices. I gasped but obediently opened my lips for her. I was powerless to resist.

"Good girl" she murmured as she fed me my own wetness.

She turned me around so that I was looking into the mirror. Her appearance was classy and elegant whereas I looked like a just-fucked streetwalker. I jumped slightly as she brushed her lips against my cheek and I felt her breath again as she pressed a card into my hand.

"Whore" she whispered in my ear.

I had to hold onto the counter to stop myself from collapsing. She was right! In the blink of an eye I'd betrayed Imma and willingly given myself to this stranger. I was a whore. And somehow that fact was incredibly exciting...

"Call me," I heard her say.

It wasn't a request. It was an instruction.

As my mind attempted to take in what had just happened, I heard her vicious stilettos clicking away. When the door closed behind her, I looked down at the business card. It contained the word Erika and a single telephone number.

And then it hit me... she hadn't even asked my name.

The party wasn't until the weekend, but I had insisted on celebrating Imma's birthday day-of, so she came over with a bottle of wine and we made pasta and laughed and watched an episode of bad reality TV.

There was a kind of pleasant buzz in Lainey's head. Somehow she had ended up on the floor, resting with her head on the arm she had stretched over the cushions. Imma was still on the opposite side of the couch, her feet tucked up underneath her as she sipped from her glass and brushed a lock of blond behind her ear.

Bottle empty, drinking their last glass each, their conversation lapsed into silence and they found themselves simply staring at each other from their positions in the room. As soon as Lainey became aware they were holding eye contact, she felt a simultaneous urge to pull away and a kind of bubbling breathlessness rising up through her legs and torso. She gulped as the kind of pins and needles excitement spread through her chest, finally breaking the stare so she could run a finger around the rim of her glass.

When Lainey's gaze raised again Imma was still contemplating her. Imma's eyes were curious, attentive, and just the start of a half-smile played on her lips. Lainey was trying to figure out how to break the silence and the tension when her lover finally spoke again.

"Do you want to play truth or dare?"

The fizzing, bubbling feeling in Lainey's body was moving down into her lower stomach, touching at the beginnings of an aching knot. "I didn't know adults played that game," she said. She'd meant it to diffuse tension, but toward the end of the sentence her voice broke in a little high-pitched hiccup that made the feeling inside her twist sharply.

"We don't have to," Imma's voice was soft in contrast to her focused gaze. As if to illustrate her laissez-faire attitude, Imma moved her legs from under herself and sat with them long over the cushions of the couch, leaning back and draping her arm over the back while she cocked her head at Lainey. One foot flexed, moved through a point, and then relaxed again. Now facing each other -- Lainey on the floor,

Imma up on the couch -- Imma's half-smile bloomed over her face into a tiny, teasing smirk.

Imma took a breath and downed the rest of her wine. "Truth or dare?"

"Truth," Lainey said. Imma felt her mind go blank -- this was why she never played this game, she thought. What was she supposed to ask?

"Um. Okay. What's the worst thing you've ever done?"

"Wow, really just diving in there." Imma said after a throaty laugh, pressing her hand to the exposed skin of her freckled chest. She was wearing a tank top over her jeans, and Lainey could see the skin just below her collarbone turn a slight shade of pink. "I cheated on a test in college once."

"That's not so bad."

"Hey, you didn't specify what kind of worst thing it had to be," Lainey said with a grin. "I got testing accommodations for my ADHD. I had this one engineering class that just...didn't make sense to me, but I needed it for my major. I studied and studied and it just wasn't coming, and so I took some notes on my graphing calculator and used them during the test. No one knew because I just got a room by myself. I still feel bad about it." She paused, looking off into a corner of the room, the fingers on her chest drumming against her skin. "Truth or dare?"

"Truth," Imma said.

"When's the last time you had sex?"

Heat rose to the woman's face. "It's been a while," she started quietly. "A couple of months, I think. Before Jenna and I broke up. Truth or dare?"

"Truth."

"Same question."

Lainey smiled. "Last week. Both laughed as it was each of them together fucking Truth or dare?"

"Truth."

"When's the last time you got off?"

Lainey's blush deepened. The warmth in her low belly that had been ebbing reignited. Breaking her gaze from Imma she looked down at the floor as she muttered, "Two days ago."

"What?" Imma said, and when Lainey looked up she saw Imma's smile had grown again. Imma was leaning toward Lainey, hand cupped around her ear in a mocking gesture. "I couldn't hear you."

Imma gave Lainey a stare that she hoped would kill, even as she felt her nipples press against the fabric of her shirt. "You heard me just fine."

"Yeah," Imma said. "But I want you to tell me again, and to look at me when you do."

Lainey shifted from side to side, trying to quiet the restlessness in her body. Their interaction was taking a sharp turn, quickly solidifying playful flirting into something more. Raising her gaze again, Lainey wished her body wouldn't give away Imma's impact on it. "Two days ago."

Imma was clearly enjoying Lainey's struggle. "In a full sentence, please."

Part of Lainey didn't know why she was going along with this. The other, growing part, was very much hoping for more. The words weren't easy to get out -- especially without breaking eye contact. Feeling the heat in her cheeks as she played into Imma's hand, she hoped Imma couldn't see the fluttering of her racing pulse against her neck. "The last time I came was two days ago."

"There you go," Imma said, the tone of her voice taking on a tiny hint of mocking condescension mixed in with the praise. "That wasn't so bad, was it? Truth or dare?"

Lainey made a sound of protest. "You just went!"

"I know," Imma said. "And now I'm going again. Truth or dare?"

"But it's my turn to ask."

Imma moved again, sliding off the couch so she was sitting on the floor next to Lainey. She made a show of slowly scooting over until they were sitting a foot or so apart, both leaning against the cushions of the couch. Imma reached forward and put the pads of her index and middle fingers under

Lainey's chin, tilting it up just slightly and running her thumb over the Lainey's jaw. "That's not the game we're playing, birthday girl. I'll ask again: truth or dare?"

Lainey tried -- really tried -- to keep her reactions in check: she tried not to flush, tried to quiet the growing ache between her legs, wished she could get her nipples to stop straining against her cotton-covered chest. Imma gently ran her thumb over Lainey's lips, eliciting a sharp intake of breath. They both knew whose rules they'd be playing by.

"Dare."

"Do you want to get a little more intense?" Imma asked. Her voice was low, and the warmth in Lainey's stomach was beginning to spread to the rest of her body. Lainey's mouth had gone dry - she gulped, nodding as Imma continued to slowly touch her face -- thumb dragging over the skin of her lips, over the ridge of her jaw, up to the sensitive skin just in front of her ear, tracing an invisible track that kept Lainey's nerves on alert for the next touch.

"Don't just nod, tell me." Imma's voice was casual -- the dominant woman I feel hopelessly in love with seemed at ease where she was sitting, like this was something she did every day with friends. Her repose made Lainey feel all the more restless.

"Yes," Lainey managed to get out.

"I dare you to take your shirt off."

Lainey shivered. Mind racing, Lainey put her hands at the bottom of her shirt, slowly bringing the fabric up over her head. She sat for a moment, topless with the shirt in her hands, unsure of what to do with it before she dropped it on the floor next to them. She wasn't wearing a bra, and her nipples stood firm and hard against her small breasts.

Imma took her time looking Lainey up and down. They lapsed into a silence again, Lainey sometimes shifting or squirming where she sat, wanting to break the silence but not quite able to get the courage up.

"You're beautiful, Lainey," Imma said finally. She still had that air of ease, a quiet kind of intention as their eyes met again. "I'd like to touch you; do you want that?"

Head swimming, Lainey nodded. After a moment and another sharp stare, she stammered, "Yes."

Imma stood up, holding out her hands to take Lainey's and pull her up. She moved gently, taking her time at positioning Lainey so she was sitting on the couch. Lainey was still in her jeans, and felt them pressing into the skin of her waist as she sat back. Imma took one of Lainey's wrists and gently guided it behind her back, then the other, before lightly scratching her nails against the skin of Lainey's upper arm and up over her shoulder. She tapped on Lainey's collarbone, tracing it with her fingers and dipping into the space between them, holding her fingers at the hollow of Lainey's throat for just a moment before tracing up and down in languid arcs.

Lainey felt like she was aware of every nerve in her body. Holding each of her arms in the opposite hand behind her back, she pressed her nails into her skin in time with the sweeping motions of Imma's hands on her chest and sides. The warm ache between her legs was undeniable, and she let out a small, soft moan as Imma's nails slowly ran up over her ribs, making goosebumps blossom over her skin.

"Truth or dare," Imma asked. Lainey struggled with the decision. Her mind had started its own journey, thinking out specific truths or dares Imma could make her face. "T-truth."

"Do you usually play with your nipples when you get yourself off?" Imma tented her hand over

Lainey's right breast so that it hovered above her puckered nipple. She swept her fingers in and out, closing and opening her palm, her fingers a tide that came close to touching Lainey's areola before ebbing out again. Lainey silently willed her lover to just touch her where she wanted to be touched, but it seemed Imma was in no rush.

"Barely ever," Lainey's voice was breathy. When she was alone she usually went straight for the prize between her legs, spending no more than a few minutes rubbing or using a toy before her thighs would clench and her toes would curl. She waited for Imma to start the next round of the game, arching her back to try and push her breast into Imma's palm.

Imma took the hint at last and slowly drew her fingers together until they brushed over the puckered skin of her areola. Deftly she played her fingers over Lainey's hard nipple, causing Lainey to gasp and shift on the couch, her legs spreading slightly, hips pushing back to try and push her chest further still into the fingertips. She enjoyed nipple play with partners, but it had rarely ever done something like this for her. This time it seemed like each light brush of Imma's fingers made something contract in Lainey's stomach and made the ache between her legs bloom even more. She was absolutely sure that she was wet. "Truth or dare?" asked Imma. Lily picked truth.

"Do you want me to pinch your nipple?" Imma asked. Lainey felt her thoughts growing cloudy. She was mentally pleading for Imma to just do these things, to just grab her and tear the rest of her clothes off and stop this game. But Imma had continued to gently play with Lainey's breast, her other hand still exploring the sensitivity of Lainey's torso. When that hand dipped down to Lainey's jeans and drew a line over where her hip met the denim, Lainey dug her fingernails hard into her arms, still holding them behind her back as she wished for more.

"Yes," she got out. "Yes. More please."

"In time," Imma said. She closed her fingers around Lainey's nipple -- quick, hard -- and Lainey gasped, her legs spreading further apart as her hips pressed back and then forward. The suddenness of it spread through her like lightning. Imma didn't stop, pinching and twisting, pulling until a sound escaped from Lainey's throat and then releasing, going back to the soft and gentle touches, back and forth between the two sensations.

When her hand came to Lainey's other breast, Lainey thought she might scream. Imma repeated the pattern there - soft and teasing, refusing to touch Lainey's nipple, then using featherlight strokes until Lainey felt her entire body screaming for more, before moving into roughness. It was only when Imma began to switch at random between twisting her nipple hard, smacking her breast, and gently rolling the flesh between her fingers until Lainey squirmed that Lainey realized being able to anticipate the pattern had been a kind of kindness.

She lost track of time. At some point, her skin so electrified that every touch and stroke and pinch made her gasp, Imma started the next round of the game. It took Lainey a full ten seconds to remember they were playing.

"Dare."

"I dare you to take me into your bedroom."

Dazed, Lainey stood up from the couch and realized where her body ached: her hips from the way she'd spread her legs on the couch; between her shoulder blades from trying to push her breasts into Imma's hands; her shoulders from holding her arms the way she had been; and of course, the place between her legs throbbed, refusing to let her ignore it.

"Truth or dare."

"Dare," Lainey said.

"I dare you to take off your clothes."

She did. Her cotton panties stuck to the wet skin of her labia as she peeled them down, and even though the heat and arousal had taken much of her self-consciousness she felt a tiny blush start up in her cheeks anyway.

"Truth or dare."

"Truth," Lainey said.

"What do you want me to do to you?"

Of course. Lainey's blush deepened. Imma had been leading so far, and it was much easier to just say yes to questions than to come out and say what she wanted. Imma was watching her closely, expression somewhat inscrutable. It didn't help that she was fully clothed, her hair barely out of place in contrast to Lainey's mental and physical mess.

"Touch me," Lainey offered finally. Imma's lips curled into a half smile, but it didn't reach her eyes. Lainey felt a touch of wetness running down one of her thighs.

"How do you want me to touch you?" Imma asked.

Lainey swallowed and let her tongue dart out to wet her lips, mouth dry. "Like...like you did out there, but between my legs."

"So, you want me to tease you?"

"Yes."

"Say that."

"I want you to tease me."

"Where?"

"M-my pussy," Lainey managed, after a moment.

"Do you want me to use my fingers?" Imma asked.

"Yes."

"What else do you want me to use?"

Lainey wanted to believe she didn't like this, didn't like feeling exposed like this, didn't like being made to ask and say so explicitly. The fact that it was taking most of her willpower to keep her hands twisting by her sides and not diving between her own legs told her something else.

"Your tongue. T-toys, if you want."

"Toys?" Imma's voice raised in a bit of amusement. "Well what do you have to offer?"

Lainey gestured toward the bed. Realizing a moment later it was less than helpful, she ambled over to it and got down on her knees, pulling out a box from underneath.

Placing the box on the bed as she stood up again, she gestured to it as she looked down at the floor.

As with everything, Imma took her time coming over to the box and looking inside. "Look at me," she said after a few minutes, and when Lainey did, Imma's grin set her arousal into overdrive all over again.

"Truth or dare," Imma said quietly.

"Dare," Lainey answered, call-and-response.

"I dare you to pick out three things from this box that you want me to use on you."

Heart fluttering against her chest, she looked through the contents, feeling Imma's eyes drilling into her. Laying the three items on the bed, she took a step back and looked back up at Imma.

They fell into a silence again, each looking at the other. It was clear Imma was waiting for something.

After a time, Imma broke the silence again. "I was going to wait for you to tell me you wanted me to use these things on you, but I'm starting to think you like feeling a little compelled."

Blood rushed to Lainey's face, her pulse pounding in her ears as Imma continued. "Are you going to be a good girl and tell me you want me to use these things on you, or do I need to dare you to do it?"

Lainey opened her mouth to speak and sputtered a bit. "I wa-- I -- I w- want to be dared."

Imma closed the gap again, reaching up to take Lainey's jaw gently in her hand. She held it there, thumb on one side and fingers on the other -- not hard, just to keep her gaze, to let her know unambiguously who was leading the show.

"This is a dare then. You're going to say what I tell you to say, do you understand?"

"Yes," Lainey said, her head swimming.

"Tell me you want me to control you," Imma said in a quiet, dangerous voice.

"I want you to control me."

"Tell me you want me to make you ache."

"I want you to make me ache."

"Tell me you want me to tease your pussy and your clit and your nipples with my tongue and my fingers and that vibrator you picked until you can barely think coherently."

Lainey was shaking, her mind reeling, stomach twisting into knots as her breath sped up. "I w-want you to tease my pussy and my clit and my nipples with your tongue and your fingers and my wand until I can barely think coherently."

Imma was smiling. "Tell me you want me to restrain you."

"I want you to restrain me."

"Tell me you want me to gag you."

"I want you to gag me."

"Tell me you want to be helpless to whatever I choose to do to you."

"I want to be helpless to whatever you choose to do to me."

"Tell me you won't come until I let you."

Lainey's breath hitched. "I won't come until you let me."

Imma's gaze and hand softened, and she brushed her thumb over Lainey's cheek. "Do you feel safe?"

Shaking, Lainey nodded. "Yes."

"Do you feel excited?"

"God. Fuck, yes."

"Do you know what to do if you don't feel safe or you need to check in?"

"Yes."

Lainey's jaw still held in her hand, Imma leaned in and gently kissed Lainey on the lips before pulling back again. "Good." She lowered her hands to Lainey's shoulders, taking her time to feel the skin there, running her fingers over her arms and down to her wrists and back up, feathering them over Lainey's chest. Then in one swift motion she put her palms flat against Lainey's chest and pushed her back onto the bed.

One set of the restraints Lainey had chosen -- simple silk sashes with hardware in the middle -- were looped over one bar in the headboard before Imma fastened an end around each wrist. Moving down her body, Imma spread Lainey's legs and anchored each ankle to the legs. Cool air pressed between her legs, reminding Lainey of the growing ache and wetness there.

Imma again seemed to be in no rush to give Lainey what she wanted. She ran her fingers over Lainey's body. It almost seemed like she was testing Lainey out -- finding all of the places that made her muscles involuntarily contract and pulse and twitch, finding which places made Lainey gasp and moan and try to tilt her hips up.

Lainey felt the bed shift and dip between her legs, and warm breath on her thigh. She strained, lifting her hips up and trying to push them down onto Imma's face. In return Imma reached under her hips and anchored Lainey's legs down, spreading them slightly as she kissed the crease of her pelvis and thigh. She bit down then, sinking her teeth hard into Lainey's inner thigh before going back to gently kissing and licking, making her way closer to her aching slit. Almost there, she hovered her mouth over Lainey's pussy and exhaled before moving to the other side and repeating, making Lainey groan and squirm and pull against her restraints.

When Imma finally ran her tongue over the length of Lainey's slit, Lainey nearly convulsed. She repeated the motion several times. She nudged Lainey's legs a little further apart, having left enough slack so that Lainey could bend them slightly. Reaching up, she put her hands on the place where Lainey's vulva met her inner thighs and pulled, spreading her lips and exposing Lainey to her tongue. She was so wet -- a surprise to neither at this point -- and the wetness coated her lips and down between her thighs. Her clit was swollen, almost twitching from its need for attention, peeking out the slightest bit behind its hood. Keeping one hand where it was to spread her open, she took her other and gently pulled up on Lainey's pubic mound, exposing the throbbing tip of Lainey's clit, and licked across it.

I'd changed my mind at least a dozen times.

I'd kept telling myself that I had no intention of calling Erika. No way. I couldn't do that to Imma. I'd never been unfaithful and I tried to convince myself that the encounter hadn't quite qualified as cheating. I'd had too much to drink and I'd been taken advantage of. After all, I hadn't done anything...

Other than let a sexy, hot, older woman finger me to the best orgasm of my life! I hadn't been able to get the encounter out of my mind and Imma had been surprised by the ferocity of my lovemaking last night. If only she'd known why.

Mind you, she probably wouldn't have remembered even if I'd confessed. We'd found a nice place for dinner and consumed far too much wine. I had my limits but Imma never knew when to stop. She'd been drunk out of her mind when we'd returned to our hotel. Maybe that had been just as well?

I'm sure I'd called her Erika when she'd gone down on me...

I couldn't get the older woman out of my mind. If she could give me such a violent climax with her fingers, what she could do with her mouth? The fantasy had me salivating. So did the thought of what it would be like to go down on her...

When morning had arrived, I'd looked at Imma beside me and then dredged up a willpower I didn't know I had. Though she was still feeling the effect of the alcohol, I'd helped her get ready and we'd headed to the conference. I reasoned that it was the only way to remove temptation and by the time we returned to our hotel this evening, Erika would be just a distant wet dream.

The plan had worked well. Until Imma had taken ill, that was. I'd seen it before. She needed to sleep off her alcoholic over indulgence and I'd managed to get her back to our hotel in a taxi and tuck her up in bed.

All I had to do was return to the conference. Instead, I'd reached for the telephone...

She worked it languidly, moving her tongue across the exposed bud while holding Lainey open. Lainey in turn pulled against her restraints, gasping at the sensation as she pressed her hips up. The reaction in Lainey was complex -- the pace wasn't nearly enough to do anything but make her want to scream and get out of the restraints and hold Imma there between her thighs. It was building something in her. She wasn't used to being touched so directly there, preferring on her own to use a vibrator above her good or else circle around her tip with her finger. It felt good -- really fucking good -- and almost too much, and yet not anything close to enough.

The light licks continued, with Imma working on her clit like it was an ice cream cone, switching between pressure and pinpoint with the tip of her tongue and broader, slower strokes that seemed to envelop her being. It wasn't long until she was shaking, sweat breaking out across her forehead as the familiar knot of tension started up. She felt her thighs squeeze, felt the muscles in her abdomen tighten as her legs strained.

Imma stopped. Pulling back, Lainey made a little whimper and pulled at her restraints, rocking her hips in the hope for more.

It didn't take long. This time Imma slipped two fingers in Lainey, curling them up to press against Lainey's g-spot. She gasped again as Imma closed her mouth around her clit, flicking her tongue back and forth over the bud and running the flat of it up it, varying her pace with the rubbing and thrusting of her fingers to keep Lainey balanced in a state of high arousal. Lainey squirmed and moaned and whimpered, clenching and twisting her hands and trying to get more -- just a little more here, or a little faster, or a little more pressure, and she'd be right at the edge.

Imma seemed to know this, and somehow worked around it, keeping Lainey aroused but not quite giving her enough to push her to where an orgasm was feasible. Lainey's nerves were alight -- she could feel everything from the stillness of the air on her chest to the tickle of Imma's hair on her abdomen. All of it made her want more.

"Imma --" she gasped, but before she could say more the woman was gone from between her legs, and something rubber was pressing against her lips.

"Did you think I forgot about this?" Imma asked quietly as she secured the gag. Lying next to Lainey, she breathed into Lainey's ear as her hand drifted down her body and between her legs again. Her fingers quickly found Lainey's clit and began to rub back and forth, lightly dancing over the tip of her exposed bundle of nerves. It made Lainey ache like almost nothing. Imma kept her lovers arousal high -- switching between rubbing her clit and thrusting two fingers inside her to rub her g-spot, which produced a deep aching need in Lainey that made her almost want to scream. She bit hard into the rubber of the gag, trying to swallow her spit but drooling around it anyway, moaning and tilting her head back. Imma wouldn't even let her get to the edge, keeping her just beneath it, somehow knowing just how to vary pressure and how much speed was needed to keep Lainey trapped in a prison of her own erotic anguish.

Lainey had long since lost her composure, pulling against the restraints and squirming and trying to thrust her hips down, fucking herself on Imma's fingers, lost in a haze of pleasure and need. Imma ground the heel of her hand into Lainey's clit and in response Lainey let out a kind of animalistic groan, followed by a series of staccato whines when the hand pulled away. The aching tension inside her was so full she thought surely at any moment it would burst. And when Imma began to manipulate her clit again, Lainey finally found herself on the edge of what she thought might be the biggest orgasm of her life. Tense, strained, the tendons of her thighs tight and visible, she trembled and tried to hold on for it.

Imma stopped. She pulled her hand away, leaving Lainey hanging on the very edge. Lainey cried out, thrusting her hips against nothing before trying to push them together and get some contact on her aching clit. Her pussy throbbed, pulsing weakly as the edge faded away, leaving in its place a feeling of sharp, desperate need.

"Did you forget?" Imma murmured in Lainey's ear. Her hand came to push back some hair from her sticky forehead. Imma's fingers went down to Lainey's nipples, playing over them, tugging and twisting and brushing to keep Lainey's body from calming down too much. "You told me you weren't going to come until I let you."

Lainey whined. Her eyes went wide. She gurgled from behind the gag, shaking her head with wide eyes, disbelieving.

Imma went back to work.

Lainey couldn't speak through the gag -- not really -- but she was sure that Imma understood the thing she was begging for. Imma didn't seem to care much whether Lainey was begging or what she was begging for, though on occasion when she worked Lainey to the very edge of orgasm she would simply say,

"No." before pulling her hand away and leaving Lainey to thrash and cry out.

It wasn't fair. It wasn't nice. Everything in Lainey's body needed to come -- her clenching, desperate, aching pussy was starting to eclipse her entire reality. Her clit throbbed -- she imagined how it must look, between her legs, a thought that on its own made her want to squirm and squeal with arousal and need.

Then Imma picked up the dildo. She held it up so that Lainey could see it and turned it on, letting its rumble fill the room. She leaned over so that they were once again peering into each other's eyes.

"Do you like this?" Imma asked, a smile on her face. Lainey, glassy-eyed, nodded.

"Do you think I should let you come?

Lainey again, nodded.

"Truth or dare?"

Lainey's breath was jagged. Around the gag, she tried to say, "Truth."

"Do you still want to be helpless to what I choose to do to you?"

Lainey nodded.

"Truth or dare."

"Truth."

"Are you aware that sometimes orgasms can be just as agonizing as edges?"

Lainey's body convulsed - one deep contraction that made her twitch. She didn't know what to say, but she felt it -- had felt the alarm bells going off in her brain at some of the previous edges, her body screaming that if she came it would feel like too much, it would be too overwhelming. She whimpered and said nothing, staring up at Imma, feeling totally exposed.

"Truth or dare," Imma said, a hint of something sinister in her voice.

"Dare," Lainey made out around the gag.

Imma leaned close so she could murmur in Lainey's ear. Her thumb flicked the switch on the dildo again, and as she pressed it lightly between Lainey's legs she let out a little chuckle. "I dare you to suffer for me."

The wand was worse. Imma made a pattern of it, lowering it and lifting it up to some rhythm that Lainey didn't know. She was so close -- closer than she'd ever been, close enough that every lift of the dildo felt like its own edge, every time it touched her she thought she just needed one more moment. She thrashed -- Imma had to sit between her legs and hold them open, putting her free hand on Lainey's pelvis to keep it down against the bed as she edged Lainey closer than Lainey thought someone could be edged.

She didn't know how long it lasted, but Imma's words bounced in her head. Each time Imma pressed the wand to her she thought it would be the last, she thought she couldn't possibly get any closer, she thought she was surely going to come, and each time it sparked a little pinpoint of fear in her of what would come on the other side of the edge.

"Do you want to come?" Imma asked, her tone almost bored as she worked her lover to near tears. Lainey nodded, whining. Imma ignored her.

"Do you want to come?" she asked again, a little later, when Lainey was nothing but a shaking mess, her world narrowing to just the edge, just that moment, trembling at the idea of what might come next. She nodded again, throwing open her eyes to try and meet Imma's . Those blue eyes bore into Lainey for a moment, considering, before going back to edging her. "Do you want to come?" she asked again. Lainey didn't know how much time had passed. She felt like she had become a personification of need. She did want to come, she needed to come, and yet each edge was sharp and jagged and left her clenching, left her a little bit scared of how intense it was going to be. She hesitated, meeting Imma's eyes again. Imma, still totally dressed, composed, holding the dildo above her vulva in an abject threat of what was still to come.

Lainey nodded, and Imma smiled. "Okay -- but if you come once, you're going to have to come three times."

Lainey whined -- a high, desperate, breathy sound gurgling out from behind the gag. She was too sensitive -- was often overly sensitive after an orgasm, and even after the edging her body felt like it was on fire. She couldn't -- surely Imma didn't expect her to -- she started to try and babble behind the gag, protesting, pulling on the restraints again.

Imma put the wand down and leaned over Lainey. She pushed hair off of Lainey's damp forehead. "Do you want to be helpless to whatever I choose to do to you?"

Lainey let out a little series of whimpers, looking up at Imma, her heart pounding, the ache between her legs consuming. Slowly she nodded.

Settling between her legs, Imma picked up the cock rocket again. Lainey felt herself stretch around two of Imma's fingers, and Imma cradled the cock in her hand against Lainey, anchored by the fingers she was using to press against Lainey's g-spot.

She flipped on the erect cock, and Lainey outright screamed. She came -- quickly, hard, so hard that her toes curled and her legs pulled against the silk sashes and her back arched and her stomach tensed. It didn't stop -- the vibrator ceaselessly buzzing against her nerves as they exploded like fireworks. She couldn't get away from it -- Imma was pushing down on her pelvis, her body keeping her legs spread, keeping her as still as she could against the cock while pushing it into her, pressing her fingers up inside of Lainey against her g-spot and rubbing firmly there.

It was too much, way too much. Lainey tried to thrash, tried to bite down, tried to do anything to get the extra energy out of her body. It hurt in a way that she loved and hated at the same time -- she wanted more, wanted to be kept right in that exact moment of floating need and overwhelm and helplessness. The cock didn't care if it was too much, and she realized Imma didn't either.

As the second orgasm built, she whined into her gag. It was too sensitive, she knew. Her pussy twitched and throbbed around Imma's fingers, still dutifully pressing into and working against her g-spot, her other hand pressing down on her pelvis to keep her still.

When the orgasm did come, it was smaller than the first, but still intense. Lainey thrashed again, pulled and tried to get away, faced the growing alarm of helplessness at the feeling of overstimulation, felt her head and mind buzz with need. It hurt, twisting inside of her, making her shake and tip her head back and thrash it side to side.

She felt Imma leaning down on top of her, pressing the cock into her body and pinning her down, murmuring in her ear again that she was doing so well, one more. Lainey listened to Imma tell her how pretty she looked like that, how desperate, how this was right where she belonged. She whimpered and cried out, her oversensitive clit trapped against the vibrating cock. She didn't want to come again -- she couldn't, it hurt, it was too much, her brain and nerves would simply not allow it.

But of course, they did. The ache grew inside her again, and she whimpered and whined and tried to get away but knew she couldn't as it pushed her again to the edge and once again over. Positively crying out, Imma clamped her hand over Lainey's mouth and the gag as her back arched, as she tried to scream, the vibrator still held against her until every contraction had wrung itself out of her pussy.

Imma clicked the vibrator off and Lainey collapsed against the bed, twitching and shaking, her breath jagged. Imma nuzzled her, gently stroking her hair and her skin, whispering how good she'd been, planting little kisses on her cheek and her shoulder.

When Lainey had completely come down, Imma undid the restraints and the gag and got up from the room, returning with some water. She slipped into the bed and pulled Lainey against her, still stroking Lainey's hair, holding Lainey against her chest.

"Good birthday present? Have fun?" she said, softly, trailing one hand over Lainey's arm, enjoying the way that her body still twitched with little aftershocks.

"Yeah," Lainey said, breathless. "We should definitely play truth or dare again sometime soon."

Imma laughed. "I'd love to. But only if we play by my rules."

Erika and I sat at the same table I'd occupied with Imma. I was sure that was a deliberate decision on her part. Returning to the same restaurant, the same table was a strong reminder of yesterday's encounter.

I hadn't eaten much. How could I? Almost as soon as we were seated she had removed one of her stilettos and begun to run her bare foot up and down my leg.

"Tell me something," she sexily murmured after coffee arrived. "Did you think of me while fucking your girlfriend last night?"

My heart began to palpitate. She instinctively knew how to turn me on.

"Of course you did," she told me as I failed to find a response. "Was it good?"

I blinked my eyes in an attempt to stop my head from spinning. This was like one of my most extreme fantasies coming to life but I had to get a grip.

"Erika, let's get something clear," I said, attempting to keep my voice calm and firm. "Imma is my girlfriend. I'm with her."

"Then why did you wait for me in the ladies yesterday?"

"I didn't... I... I..."

"You acted like the whore you are, darling. You can lie to me but you can't lie to yourself. That's why you

called and asked to meet today,
isn't it?"

She placed her elbow on the table
and rested her chin on her hand,
so casually that would could have
been talking about the menu. Her
foot under the table rose higher
and began to push my legs apart.

"You know what's going to
happen..." she drawled. "I'm going
to bring alive every sluttish fantasy
you've ever had, don't you?"

My hair stood on end and
goosebumps appeared on every
part of my body, but she hadn't
finished. Her foot was scraping
along my inner thigh and her eyes
refused to leave mine.

"I'm going to crawl inside that pretty
head and peel you apart..."

I shuffled on the chair, knowing I should put a stop to this before it went too far but my legs were widening of their own volition. It felt as if she understood my desires better than I knew them myself.

"Give me your panties."

I gasped. Was she joking?

"Now! Here, at the table. No one can see." She stretched out her hand. "Take them off and give them to me, dear."

The way she looked at me, the way she spoke, made me feel powerless to do anything other than follow her instruction. A blush spread across my cheeks as I shifted my body and slid the skimpy panties down my legs. I was as discreet as I could manage

but didn't dare glance around in
case anyone was watching.

Erika took the black panties from
my trembling hand and placed
them in open view on the table
beside her. Her foot found my
wetness and she ran her big toe
along the full length of my opening.

"You can't cum. Understand?"

Her toe gently parted my labia and
I stifled a groan. When she eased
the toe inside me, my body was
consumed with a dizzying heat.
Sweat broke out on my forehead.
Imma loved sex in public places
but she was an amateur compared
to this woman.

When she somehow rotated her
toe, my body jerked like a
marionette being yanked to the

ceiling. She smiled, giving me time to recover and then obtained the same result by repeating the action. I whimpered and held a serviette to my lips, trying to stifle the sound. Erika's eyes sparkled with amusement.

"Whore," she mouthed to me, twisting the toe inside me again.

The orgasm hit me like a freight train. My entire body began to shudder. I knew that my predicament would be clear to anyone observing us and yet I couldn't hold back the spellbinding climax. Erika kept her big toe in position, gently moving it inside me as if pacing me down from the throbbing intensity.

"Didn't I tell you that you mustn't cum," she eventually murmured, playful shaking an admonishing finger. "I think we're going to have to punish you when we get to my house, don't you? By the way, what's your name, dear?"

Erika's home was amazing—large, spacious and full of light. But I had no time to admire it. Her hands were on my body as soon as we entered, sliding my dress from my shoulders. I hadn't worn a bra and she nodded her approval as she stood back to admire my body, naked except for the nude thigh high stockings.

"It's just as well that my husband is away," she smiled. "I think he would have a conniption if he knew there were two whores in the house."

Turning, she walked across to the centre of the room and then turned back towards me. Leaning against the back of an antique looking sofa, she sexily crooked a finger.

"Come here."

Her voice was low and husky, as if the anticipation of what was about to happen was getting to her, too. When I was a couple of feet away, she slowly gathered and then pulled up the hem of her dress.

"Take off my panties, there's a good girl."

Her left hand found my right shoulder and applied a little downward pressure. I obediently sank to my knees, hooking my fingers into her panties as I did. I kept my gaze fixed upwards on hers as I gently pulled them down her legs.

She lifted one leg and then the other to help me drag them away.

"Such a polite little slut..." she murmured, reaching down and stroking under my chin. "It's time now. Why don't you show me what you can do..."

I felt dizzy, like a drug addict needing their fix. Dipping my head forwards, I ran my tongue over my lips and then licked along the inside of her thigh.

"Oh yes... good girl..."

I marveled at the softness of her skin as I lifted one of her toned legs and carefully placed across my shoulder. That gave me a better angle and for a few moments I worshipped her beautiful pussy with only my eyes and my breath. The spell was broken when Erika's reached down to grasp my long dark hair. Her nails gently scratched my scalp as she pulled me to the Promised Land.

"It was my cunt you were thinking about when you were in bed with your girlfriend last night, yes?" Her voice was thick with need. "Lick me, Baby..."

The words had hardly escaped her lips when I attacked her with my mouth. I needed to feed and I couldn't hold back. Electricity ran through my body at the first lap of my tongue. I licked my lips, savoring her taste, and then returned for more.

I indulged myself for a while, luxuriating in the sound of her soft moans, and then traced a path between her labia with my tongue. They yielded gently and she mumbled unintelligibly as she fractionally adjusted her position against the sofa. Her clutching hands kept my face pressed firmly in position.

I gripped her thighs more tightly with my hands and pushed my tongue forward. There was a slight resistance but then it entered her with startling ease. I almost creamed on the spot. I felt heat, moisture, taste, aroma and an incredible silkiness.

Erika moaned and I felt a gentle but insistent pressure on my tongue. It was as if she was moulded around me, as if we were intended for one another.

I flexed my tongue inside her and felt her swell slightly to accommodate me. Her body was inviting me even deeper and her muscles were trying to suck me in. What was it she'd said earlier?

She wanted to crawl into my head and peel me apart?

Her grip on my hair tightened. She was growling now and rubbed my face up and down her wet pussy, using me for her pleasure. She moved slowly, smothering her juices across my forehead, nose, mouth and chin. I was her personal fucktoy...

I don't know how long she used me but I didn't want the moment to end. Maybe I should have felt humiliated, degraded, but instead I was very, very aroused. Eventually, she dragged my head away and stared down into my eyes.

"I could drown you..."

My pussy flooded with arousal. Yes. Oh, Yes!!

I tried to jam my head back between her thighs but her stiletto heel stopped me. She placed it against my chest and with a grunt sent me tumbling backwards onto the carpet. For a few seconds I looked up at her, shocked, eyes wide.

Her chest was rising and falling as she pushed upright and reached behind her body. Before I knew what she was doing, she had released her dress and allowed it to crumple around her ankles. My breath caught in my throat.

She stood before me in her corset, stockings and sharp black patent pumps—a sexual Goddess displaying herself to her conquest!

The heat inside my body was almost overwhelming me. She was sex incarnate.

Then she was stepping across my prone body, placing a long leg either side of me and slowly kneeling over my face. I thought my heart was going to explode. I just stared up at her—a puppet on her string—as she lowered herself, resting on her palms and knees as she squatted on all fours just above my head.

"Keep your head on the floor and arms by your sides," her voice barked down at me. "I want you to watch."

I nodded. It was impossible to speak. I could hardly breathe.

Her right hand slid slowly down her stomach. I could clearly see the backs of her knuckles as her fingers reached her sex. It was beautiful, with just a tiny tuft of hair adorning the top, and her musky odour was intoxicating.

A growling sound came from the back of her throat as she tilted her head back. Eyes closed, she slid her two middle fingers inside her wetness.

I stared disbelievingly as she began to fuck herself just inches away from my face. Her actions were so unexpected, so raw, that I was instantly captivated, an innocent bystander who was now a prisoner in her sexual world.

She moved her fingers gently at first, her face betraying her pleasure, and as the tension mounted she began to thrust harder, deeper. The wet sound, her musky aroma, and the lewd sight just a fraction away was overwhelming. I wanted to raise my hands and drag her down onto my mouth but her instructions had been clear. Each time her fingers withdrew I could see her inner lips gripping them, as if they didn't want to feel the void for any longer than necessary.

"Want to taste?" she murmured, looking down at me again.

She removed both fingers and held them up to the light. I thought she was going to make me beg but then she smiled and wiped them across my lips. I lapped at them like a rabid beast, up and down and then at the flesh between her fingers. When she eventually withdrew them from my mouth, I continued to run my tongue back and forward across my lips to savor the taste.

When she worked both fingers back inside herself and then added a third, I whimpered like a baby. God, I so wanted that cunt...

"Last night..." She shuddered slightly as she spoke. Her voice was hoarse. "I thought of you while I let my husband fuck me. Just as you were thinking of me..."

Her free hand reached for my hair, gathering it between her clutching fingers. She raised my head up so that she could smear herself across my face again.

"Is this what you were thinking of?" she husked. "Suck it... Suck my peach..."

My mouth attacked her pussy like a thirsty woman lost in the desert. I wrapped my hands around her thighs, dragging her even closer. She placed her palms over them, entwining our fingers. I was so aroused I thought I might go out of my mind. I couldn't get enough— sucking, licking and lapping as if I would never feed again.

"Does your girlfriend excite you like this, Lover dear?"

I heard her provocative words and responded by running my tongue across her clit. I was out of control and we both knew it.

"Goddddd, yesss," she moaned as I flicked my tongue at her clit. Over and over again. "You delightful bitch! Bite... Bite, damn you..."

We gave ourselves to each other in our different ways, two animals in the wild venting their need in the wildest, lewdest fashion. Erika held my head motionless with one hand as she rotated her hips in slow circles on my face. Her other hand rose up to her magnificent breasts, pinching and pulling at her left nipple. She smothered me, rising occasionally to let me breathe and then grinding again.

I needed her climax, but just as I thought it was within my grasp she was twisting her body around. With a remarkable dexterity, she reversed her position and I understood what she had in mind. Imma and I loved to Sixty Nine but right here, right now, this woman was taking me into a different world.

Her hands slithered under me to cup my ass and pull me to her mouth. I gasped out loud. The sound turned into a scream as she traced the letter "E" onto my labia. Where the fuck had she learnt that? She took her time on each side, as if she were branding me with the heat of her tongue. There was no respite and I didn't care. Her mouth had found my clit and her tongue was tracing the letter again.

"Oh My God... Erika..."

I heard her mutter something in response but all I could focus on was her pleasuring mouth and the orgasm that wasn't far away. Erika understood my need. She was an expert, after all. Her head drew away for a second and just as I was about to whimper out a complaint, she dove forward again and impaled me with her tongue.

"OH GOD..." The words came out like a scream.

Her tongue dove even deeper. Her chin bounced against my clit. Her mouth was treating my pussy the way her cunt had treated my face. Her movements were fast, frantic and deliberate. I felt the tide sweeping in. So did she.

"Cum for me, slut..."

Her words bounced around my head.

"Cum now..."

Oh God! I pumped my hips against her face.

"Spray me, bitch. SPRAY ME!!"

An uncontrollable scream tore from my parched throat. For the first time in my life, I squirted.

The first gush hit her full force, splashing across her face. She moaned her approval and opened her mouth to accept the second blast. My entire body was shuddering and I couldn't stop. She plastered herself against me, pinning my body to the floor as a third gush violently released itself. This time she almost choked as she frantically tried to catch and swallow it all.

I could feel her sharp manicured nails digging into my skin and I had no idea how long she continued to lap at my juices. Another orgasm was seeking me out and behind my closed eyelids, darkness was closing in...

*

I woke up in a strange bed in a strange room. My naked body was lying on top of the crumpled white satin sheets. As reality returned, I sat up hurriedly and covered my mouth as I saw the darkness outside the window.

How long had I been here?

One by one, memories of the afternoon reappeared inside my head like a series of video clips from a porn movie. I had a vague recollection of Erika helping me to her bedroom. She'd scissored me and I'd screamed like a banshee when I'd climaxed. I had thought that Imma was the best at tribbing but this woman easily worked a couple more screaming orgasms from me before succumbing to her own.

I glanced around the empty bedroom and caught my reflection in the dressing table mirror. I looked a mess. My sweat-covered hair was practically sticking to my scalp and I tried to pull it into some sort of shape with my fingers. It occurred to me that this was what a whore must look like when she had been used.

That's what I had been. Erika's whore!

My body jumped when the bathroom door opened. Erika stood there, posing sexily in the doorway, as naked as the day she was born. The knowing smile on her face had become familiar. But it was the large strap-on fastened around her hips that shocked me. She began to stroke it with her hand as I stared across the room.

"I thought I might be able to persuade you to stay the night," she huskily told me, pushing away from the doorframe.

The dildo flapped lewdly in front of her as she sauntered across the room towards me. Once she reached the bed, she crawled up beside me on the sheets.

I knew I couldn't stay any longer. Imma would be wondering where I was. It was time to put an end to this and take my leave. Wasn't it? But Erika's hand had found my hair and she was tugging my head towards the phallus.

My eyes glanced up into hers as she rubbed the head against my mouth. I groaned and then opened my lips. It was a long time since I'd had any sort of cock. Erika gave an approving moan as I spat saliva onto the long shaft and then began to suck.

She patted my head. "Tomorrow, I think we might go to meet Imma...I mean after all she is my best friend"